STOCK OPTIONS

The Best Proven Strategies To Safely Invest And Avoid The Most Common Mistakes

Adrian McNulty

© Copyright 2018 by Adrian McNulty - All rights reserved.

It is not legal to reproduce, duplicate, or transmit any part of this document in either electronic means or in printed format. Recording of this publication is strictly prohibited.

Table of Contents

Introduction 7

Chapter 1: Stock Options, What You Need To Know Right Off The Bat ………………………………….. 11

Chapter 2: Key To Success …………………..... 25

Chapter 3: Common Trading Strategies ………….... 39

Chapter 4: Option Volume And Open Interest, Option Liquidity, And Option Time Value …………………73

Chapter 5: Last Tips ………………………….. 86

Introduction

Most employees have stock option as a major component of their separate compensation packages, most of these individuals only understand the basic aspects of their stock options. This book will educate you about investing in stock options and the best strategies to use when it comes to trading stocks.

Stock option is believed to have started in ancient times, where agricultural products were used. Unfortunately, it was not very popular like stocks because of insufficient marketing. Getting option sellers was very difficult, although there were buyers. Trading option started when CBOT (Chicago Board of Trade) came into existence, which was 1848. Later on, other exchanges like New York Cotton Exchange, Kansas City Board of Trade and Minneapolis Grain Exchange came into existence. At around 1968 CBOE (Chicago Board Options Exchange) was formed, which facilitated liquidity of options. At first CBOE was set up for option trading only. In the 70s put option had grew in importance and they started to trade as well.

The SPX begun index options on Chicago Board Options Exchange. Having seen the growth of option trading, other exchanges like NASDAQ and NYSE also started trading stock in 1985.

Self-Discipline: The Perfect Tool To Success

On a daily basis, the stock market is usually governed mostly by fear and greed. This is usually seen by market going up several points one day and falling the next day. In some cases, this volatility can be seen on the same day. The famous market gurus, acquaintances, friends and stockbrokers can easily influence you in different ways. A stockbroker can make you excited over a phone call telling you the stock market is going to shoot up or go down. This statement should not get you excited even for a second. A good stockbroker should only tell you if the stock market has gone down or up. There is no one on earth who can exactly predict the market movements. If you want to make something out of trading stock, invest in stocks, which are long term. I am still waiting to see a stock trader who is a short term and he/she has been able to retain earnings for long time.

Short-term market movements mostly tend to behave in an irrational manner. The reason to this is very simple, on short-term basis it is highly likely that the market is controlled by psychological forces. Scientists are yet to discover an instrument that can measure or predict the psychology of humans. Therefore, your miscalculated strategies are bound to be correct one/two times. Once you have been able to generate some cash using these strategies, you start becoming a victim of your own wrong deeds. At some point, you will end up losing all your gains and even more.

When it comes to trading stock the hardest part is killing your ego. I can assure you, your ego is one of the biggest force that can lead to disaster. Before someone place an order to trade he/she needs to convince themselves that the market might lead their stock in the other direction and at that time they do not know the market direction. A trader is bound to be right at some period or another. When you get it right, you incline to forget how many times you were wrong. Although, this is human nature.

Be fearful. You should sell when a lot of people are buying. Be greedy. You should buy when most individuals are selling. I don't necessarily mean that you always have to buy when the marketing is falling or sell every time when your market is going up. No matter what, always stick to your original principles of stock trading. Your daily life or moods should never be governed by Dow Jones's graphs.

Having said all this, if you do not have self-discipline, I will advise you not to trade in stock market. When it comes to trading, you need to develop self-discipline, which will allow you to control your fear and greed.

Chapter 1: Stock Options, What You Need To Know Right Off The Bat

Having an option makes you an owner of a contract, which gives you the right to either sell or buy a security. You can do this at a particular price and time but you are not obligated to. As an investor, you are able to sell and buy options just like in the case of stocks.

The Basic Types Of Options

- **The Call Option**

With the call option, you are able to purchase the fundamental security at a particular price and time. You can buy a call option in case you expect the prices of the fundamental security to go up before an option expires. As an owner of an option you can trade it for a profit, not having to actually buy a share of stock.

In the instance where you figured it wrongly and the stock dropped from the original price. Let the option expire, this will result to you making a loss of the cost of the option only. Investors use the call option for income generation, speculation and tax management.

- **The Put Option**

The put option gives you the right to sell the fundamental security at a certain time and price. If the put option price is going down, you can purchase it before it expires.

Basic Facts About Options

- An option expires on the expiration date which is the third Friday of the month. The option can expire on Thursday in case Friday is a holiday.
- Options are sold in 100 shares lots although they are quoted per share.
- Not to forget the strike price, this is the basic security that you can sell or buy as a complete option contract.

Understanding the price and vesting options is important. When it comes to vesting, you have the right of buying options for a period of time. What is the vesting schedule? How long can you buy the vested options? These are some questions you ought to consider.

Stock options are intended to be valueless by most companies, so as to not create a taxable event with the Internal Revenue Service. As a result, there is no need to inform you that the fair market value for an option on the date of the grant is very important. This is the reason of hiding the income effect of the granting option, which is priced lower than the fair market value.

Are you ready to pay taxes? With stock options, you need to be ready to pay taxes. When it comes to premise fundamental stock option value, you are able to purchase stock in future at the current low price. Therefore, when you exercise the option you are accountable to pay taxes associated with the profit made.

When your options are becoming more valuable with time, consider tomorrow's options. They will become hard and scarce for you continue in the results. Therefore, consider the moment always and keep in mind that the moment of getting stock options is now.

Understanding Stock Option Basics

As an investor, you have strategies available from the adaptability of options stems.

- **Buying Calls**

The call option contract enables its holder to have the right of buying a specified number of shares. The shares are fundamental stock at a given strike price that is before the contract expires. The following are reasons for buying calls:

- Buying calls in order to participate in the upward movements. Buying stocks at a fixed price is more valuable for the price of underlying stocks rises. Hence, you'll have two picks of disposing in-the-money option which are:
- Sell the option contract at $550 which will result to you losing your position. Collect the

difference between the paid premium and received premium $200. You will end up making a profit of 57% while given a similar price movement in a stock purchase your profit would be 10%.

- Exercise your option by buying for instance the underlying ABC stock at $50 per share which comes to $5,350. Then sell the shares on the stock market, you will end up making a total of $5500. Making a net profit of $150.

Profitability depends on the time remaining before the expiration dates affects the premium.

- **Buying Calls As Part Of Your Investment Plan**

The 90/10 strategy is used, which involves enlisting 10% of your investments funds in purchased call. The rest that is 90% in money market instrument that is held until the expiration of the option. This strategy has an influence from the options and limited risk. This allows investors to benefit promising stock price move. The downside risk is limited which is from the call premium minus interest earned which is on the T-bills.

- **Buying Calls To Lock In A Stock Purchase Price**

As an investor, you see an attractive opportunity but you do not have the required cash flow at the moment. Well then, you can use the call option in order to lock in the purchasing price. This can be for as long as eight months.

- **Buying Calls To Evade Short Stock Sales**

By purchasing the call option, you can limit a possible loss that is due to occur, when you sold your stock with an anticipation of a decline in price. Shorting stock needs a margin account plus a margin calls which can force you to liquidate your position hastily.

A call option cannot be used to protect the option owner against any additional margin calls or even premature liquidation of short stock position. It can be used to offset the short stock position upside risk. . Nonetheless, this decision is risky for in the event your stock price falls after exercising, your stock option could be worthless. You may still have to pay an alternative minimum tax.

Exercising Your Stock Option

Having a process-drive is very important when you are evaluating the stock options. This enables you to make smarter financial decisions. Here are some questions to help you in evaluating stock options:

- **What Is Uncle Sam's Cut?**

Do you earn a high income? Earning a high income, exercising plus selling your options within the same year, leads to the stock being highly taxed. At a rate of 25% federal all the way up to 39.6% with your state's tax. In case you have an income that is variable and there is a possibility for a lower income going forward. This can sway you to wait then sell when you will have a lower tax imposed on you.

In the case where your options are expiring, you may not have a choice. You can rather spread your options over several years in order to stay at a lower tax bracket.

After exercising, put into consideration how long you want to hold onto the stock. If you are able to hold stocks for more than a year, then they qualify for the capital gain taxes. This tax has a lower rate than ordinary tax rates. Therefore, you need to know if you're Incentive Stock Options (ISO) or the Nonqualified Stock Options (NQSO) is vital.

After exercising any gains that results from an ISO and held for a year is taxed at capital gain rate. Be cautious as there may be a difference in grant price and fair market value while exercising. This is used in AMT calculation as it is known as a bargaining element.

- **How Big Is Too Big?**

Options easily become the largest holding in portfolio when stock prices begin to increase. Due to its grant price, an option has a big influence. As a result, they can remain to be worthless for years only to rise suddenly and drastically when a company's share becomes a hot commodity.

Hence, a concentration risk is considered so that a lot of your portfolio is not dependent on fluctuation of prices. Put into consideration the valuation metrics plus future growth potential of stocks. If your stock is above 10% of overall investment portfolio, then you ought to cut off some exposure.

- **When Do They Vest?**

It is vital for you to know when you will be acquiring the shares. Although you have options that are granted, this does not mean that you have obtained an immediate bonus. A typical vesting schedule ought to be over four years, with a quarter of shares vesting on every year. When the shares are vested, exercised and then you can sell them.

- **What's The Potential?**

Be careful of the partiality you may have in line with your company's growth prospects, for you are still working at the company. You can spend some time in investigating all the fundamentals of the company's stock. This you can do by finding someone who will help you in decision–making.

Add the analysis of the current valuation metrics which includes: P/E ratio, high quality measures, P/S ratio and risk measures, all these needs to be part of your decision making. You can ask questions like:

- How profitable is the company?
- How quickly are the sales growing?
- Who else is the owner of the stocks?

- What type of competition does the company have?

Understanding The Right Nature Of Your Stock Option

Options signify a contract between a seller and a buyer. As a seller you have the mandate of either buying or selling stock to buyers at a stated price and time. On the other hand, as a buyer you have the right to complete the transaction before the specified time, but you are not obligated to. Check for the following features in a stock option.

i) Expiration Date

All the options expire after a period of time. Once it expires, your right of exercising does not exists anymore leading to stock becoming worthless. Each option contract has an expiration month which is specific. To know the specific date when expiration occurs is dependent on the type of option.

Example we see that stock options, which are listed in the United States expires on the third Friday of the month. This is when it's to expire.

Most options in companies contain a 10 years of life. Therefore, do not act too quickly, for this will result in you losing the benefits of your execution strategy. Do not have a lot of your net worth being tied up just in one company stock. Instead diversify your risk, spread your asset holdings to different types of stocks.

ii) Underlying Asset

This is a security where as an option seller you have an obligation of delivering or purchasing from an option owner when the option is exercised. When it comes to stock options, the fundamental assets are the specific shares of a company. Options are also available in form of: indices, currencies and commodities.

iii) Option Type

We have two options types which include: the non-qualified stock option and the qualified option. The qualified option is also known as incentive stock option (ISO), which is limited to the employees. The tax treatment depends on the type of option that you are holding.

A qualified option contains tax attributes, which allows you to be able to delay in paying tax at the moment of exercise. You may also be able to pay your taxes at a low capital gains rate. As a holder of an option, it's important for you to decide whether or not you are going to sell the shares you have exercised, or if you are going to hold on the exercised shares.

In case you sell the shares immediately, you are bound to pay the exercise price money and ordinary tax rates. At the difference of your exercising price with the FMV that is at the time of exercise. This is applicable for both non-qualified and qualified shares. Exercising and selling the shares immediately results to income are being deemed as ordinary income in the two awards.

Comparing Stock Option To Actual Shares Of Stock

Similarities Between Option And Actual Shares Of Stock

- Option investors like actual share investors, possess the ability to follow trading volume, price movements and other pertinent information for day to day or minute by minute. The seller or buyer is able to learn the price for his order.

- Both options and stocks are examples of listed securities. Orders for buying and selling options are handled by brokers the same way as orders to sell and buy stocks. The listed option orders are performed on the trading floors of the national SEC-regulated exchanges. Here trading is done in an open, competitive market.

- Like actual shares of stocks options trade with traders making bids (buyers) and sellers who are making offers. In actual share the bids and the offers are for shares of stock. While in options the bids plus offers are the rights to be able to buy or sell 100 shares per option contract.

The Differences Between Options And Actual Shares Of Stocks

- Options do not have a fixed number whereas there are numbers in actual shares. An option is a contract which involves a buyer who is willing to pay a price in order to have certain rights. The seller is willing to grant the buyer with these rights for a price. While in actual shares stocks, the number of outstanding open interest is dependent on the number of buyers plus sellers who are interested in receiving and deliberating on these rights.

- Option has limited life. Actual share stock can be retained indefinitely with the hope of increasing in its value. Yet every option has an expiration date. In the case of an option, if it's neither closed out nor exercised before its expiration, it ceases to be a financial instrument.
- Actual share stock owners have a share in the company, some voting rights plus rights to dividends. Option stock owners on the other hand take part in the potential benefit of the stock's price movement.
- Options are certificateless unlike actual share stock which has certificates as evidence of their ownership. An option indicates its positions by printing statements prepared by brokerage firm of buyers or sellers.

Chapter 2: Key To Success

The key to success is focusing on stocks which matter. It's also important to note that there isn't a right or a wrong way of analyzing stock. We have specific fundamentals elements that need to be paid attention to. You also need to know when to "cut your losses short and make your winners run". Hence you need to know when to sell.

Having a strategy is very important as this helps to sell your stock for a profit. When your target is reached you can sell. Remember the most important fact in making a success with your stock is focusing on stocks that matter. Also stocks do not tend to bounce back.

Components That Matter When It Comes To Stock Success

    i.   Keeping a trading diary – this will help you be able to recognize trades plus patterns which are successful. Therefore, you do not need to be overwhelmed by what you see as random data. The diary helps you to improve on what is working for you and be able to continue in the trade.

ii. The PE ratio is a very important element that needs to be assessed when you look into stock value. This is the price of the stock's share which is divided by its earnings of that share. The result ratio is used to determine the value of a company, plus the amount of dollar the company earns. How much the investors are willing to pay for the dollar. A high PE indicates that a company expects future growth.

iii. You can beta test the stock, as beta shows the unpredictability of a stock. A high beta number indicates how unpredictable it is. Beta numbers are found next to PE ratio. A beta number which is higher than one shows that the stock rises and drops often.

iv. Check the debt equity ratio which is used to determine a company's leverage. This is obtained by dividing all the company's liabilities by the equity of stockholders. This ratio shows how a company is financing its assets and when a company is moving into a debt. Therefore, avoid high numbers.

v. The above mentioned factors are important but don't have a narrow focus by looking at the mentioned factors only, for it will result into a shorten insight. Hence, consider multiple factors while choosing a stock to put your energy to.

Key Things To Succeed In Your Stocks

- **Think Long Term**

Short term trading is a big loser game for investors. This explains why taxes and buying or selling shares on quarterly earnings are not for average Joes' to invest in. It's rather for automated trading platforms.

Good opportunities for stock trading are when a stock is laid off by the market. It deteriorates despite the steady economic outcomes which will produce a long course of profits. Transportation stocks which includes railroads and airlines go through a long-out-of favor stretches. They later churn out sizeable gains when the industry dynamics and economic conditions align.

For instance, due to years of mismanagement, airline industry went to bankruptcy in 2000s. This resulted to the merger wave which leads to more competition and balance. The American Airlines, Delta Air Lines and United Continental benefited from reducing the fuel costs.

It is important that you understand what you want to achieve in the long run. Therefore, have a plan that will help you to achieve your desires.

- **Get Familiar With The Filings**

Some investors tend to think that they have six senses to help them in getting good companies. Most of the investors though have to do their homework. The best point to start is the SEC where there are regular fillings by public companies.

The companies are required to put in details of the company's finances to its potential risk factors and conflicts. The annual 10-K has a lot of information that ranges from quarterly to annual financial numbers. The description of the business lines, its management explanation on the growth costs and opportunities. Regulatory filings will have detail information on management changes, stock transactions and acquisitions by the board members.

Avoid aimless choosing of stocks as blind picks usually lead to a lot of risks in investing in the marketplace. Research on specific companies that, you are going to invest in. Thus ensuring that, you are investing on a reliable company. Have a few years of the company's health as this is a good indicator of how they are doing financially.

- **Noticing A Downturn**

When you invest you do not want to lose your money. When you notice that one of your stocks is constantly decreasing, you will have a lesser risk of jumping ship early. This will allow you to make new investment elsewhere rather than waiting for success in the long run. Constant building of the portfolio results to more success and eventually more money.

Why Selling Is Key To Success

Selling puts is profitable especially in the long run. This is evident in academic researches. The reasons are:

- The options tend to be priced at a fair value. This is a very well-known variance premium. As a result, this can be enough to make selling of the puts profitable. Even if there is no upward drift of underlings.

- The equity market has gone up consistently in the past 40 years. This is also the period that stock options have been listed on exchanges list.

It's important to choose the right time to sell your stock. This can be a difficult task as most trades find it hard to, separate their emotions from their own trades. The emotions of greed plus the fear or regret can be a big setback for traders. Therefore, the key to being a successful trader is managing these emotions. Selling your stocks at the right time can make you obtain a fortune of your own.

Things To Consider When Selling

1) Rising Profits

Most investors do not sell when stock rises from 10% to 20%. This is because they do not want to miss on more returns in case the stock shoots all the way to the moon. We can see that the investors here are governed by their emotions of greed. As they tend to hope that their stock will be a big winner. On the other side, if there is 10% or 20% fall in the stock, investors will still not sell their stock due to the fear of regret in case their stock rebounds.

So when should you sell your stock? For you to do this you need to separate your emotions and make selling of your stock as mechanical as possible.

2) Valuation-level Sell

Here an investor sells their stock when it reaches the valuation range or target. The common valuation metrics used here includes: PE ratio and price-to-sales. This approach is common in value investors who get stocks which are undervalued. It is a good signal to sell stocks when they become overvalued.

3) Opportunity Cost

An investor has portfolio of stocks, he would sale the stock when an opportunity avails itself. This method requires a constant monitoring, research plus analysis of your portfolios and any potential stock additions. When a better investment is recognized, an investor is to eliminate a position in the current holding that is not promising.

4) Deteriorating Fundamental Sell

This rule triggers a sale of certain fundamental in a company's financial statement, when it falls below certain levels. This sell strategy is a bit similar to opportunity cost, because the stock sold basing on the previous strategy has deteriorated. When selling a stock basing on deteriorating fundamentals, traders usually focus on the balance sheet which emphases on coverage ratios and liquidity.

Most people lose their money in buying whether it's on call or put option. Option traders do not put in account facts about derivatives markets, which are – most options expire that is they become "out-of-the-money". Means buyers tend to lose on option trades. A serious option trader needs to formulate a new option writing method in order to get the best from a market.

Reasons For "Out-Of-The-Money"

- The share of calls and puts which expired-worthless was influenced by the primary trend of an underlying market.

- Nearly 3 out of 4 options are held till expiration thus becoming worthless.

- Option buyers are coming out ahead even when sellers are going against the trend.

Reasons For Selling

1) Not Controlled By Greed

Buying options tend to be because of greed as you do not know when the trend will reverse itself. This can result to you selling the option too late. To avoid this, you can sell put options, as its worst case could be you own a stock at a lower price than what you might have intended to.

2) Earn Interest On Other's Money

Selling of options earns you money, although you may not be able to withdraw the money. You will continue to earn interest with the money until expiration. With this in mind, you need to be careful in selecting a brokerage. As a majority of brokerage companies do not pay any interest on the money that is accumulated on the selling option.

3) Time In Your Favor

Having time on your favor is the biggest advantage you have when it comes to selling options. We know that each option has two values which are time value and the intrinsic value. You can have a case where a stock is not moving against the trend, this may be so but the time value on the stock will be eroding every day. As a result, the option is of a lesser value as days goes on when you sell the option, the seller gains everyday on the stock.

4) Stop Losses

You can put stop losses either above or below a particular price when you buy options. This can be done on fundamental analysis or technical analysis. When selling puts, you do not need to have a stop loss for the worst case will result in you owning stock at the price which you intended to.

5) Shared Risk

The advantage of selling your stock in order to raise funds is when your company fails you won't have to pay back the investors. Therefore, you don't suffer lose alone. Although you could get sued in case you were negligent with the use of the money, investors take the risk of losses as when you take the loss in investing in your company. Equity financing is the way to go to minimize your potential loss.

The Downside Of Selling Options

1) Loss Of Ownership

Loss of ownership is one the major downside of selling stocks. This is because you are giving up ownership to your stock. Investors invest into companies with the hope of profiting when the company succeeds and able to generate profits with time. Small business owners are seeking equity financing without having to contemplate the certainties of the new ownership.

Giving up part of your company in order to get investments can be very frustrating. As profits from your hard work is diminished. Some capitalists ask for preferred stock which has superiority over common stock that is owned by the founders. Therefore, the preferred shares are paid first thus leading to you as an owner receiving less return.

2) Unlimited Risk

As an investor the maximum risk you will get for losing your money is equivalent to the amount of money that you used in purchasing the option. Also a seller will have the maximum risk to be equivalent to amount of money he/she sold the option for. The seller has a risk of buying back the stock at a higher price.

As investors seek to reduce risk by careful selection of investments opportunities, which will lead to getting bigger returns. Losses are bound to occur but as a trader the ultimate goal is being able to shift the ratio of winners-to-losers. Thus favoring profitable and strong portfolio returns.

The selling of naked calls amounts to unlimited risks. Hence, such strategies are appropriate for urbane traders who have discipline and proper risk management, because of the limitless losses.

Naked selling of the put options can be very dangerous when there is a fall in the stock price. The option seller will be forced at a certain price to buy the stock. The lowest level a stock can drop is zero, thus giving the losers a floor to land on. In call options, how high a stock can climb is limitless. This means the potential losses that one can get is limitless.

3) Loss Of Control

In line with loss of ownership, you are also relinquishing some control on your stock. This is because, some investors insist on getting representative work or becoming part of your board. You can avoid this by spreading your stock sales to a few investors therefore able to keep decision-making power. The higher the ownership stakes the higher the control influence on decisions of the company.

Other downsides of selling your stocks are the following. You are bound to occasionally lose a lot of money. This is largely alleviated by trade sizing, as trying to make 20% in a year is sensible but trying to make the 20% in a month is dangerous. You will suffer a lot of regret, when the stocks go up your regret will be of not buying the stock entirely.

Chapter 3: Common Trading Strategies

There are three option trading strategies that in investor can utilize to yield profit. Investors either buy or sell puts and call options in the market. The method of choice of an investor determines the maximum profit or loses he is likely to make and the breakeven points of the trade. An investor should be careful when choosing a strategy that best suits his trade needs.

1) Bullish Strategies

Traders who utilize Bullish strategies are bullish Investors. They believe that the stoke price will increase overtime. They believe they have the right to purchase stock at the strike price. A Bullish investor can sell puts or buy calls. The seller of a put believes the stoke price will rise because his obligation is to buy the stock. Bullish investors can be very bullish, moderately bullish or slightly bullish. Very bullish strategy is the simple call buying strategy used by beginners who do not know so much about option trade.

Moderately bullish trading strategy allows the user to aim a price for the underlying stock and utilize bull spreads to reduce risk of loses. It gets high users because it is a less costly strategy and is able to yield a lot of profit. Mild bullish strategies are stock strategies that generate money provided the underlying stock does not fall on options that have a near expiry date. It is necessary to assess how high the stock price will occur in order to select the optimum trading strategy. The two most commonly used bullish strategies are the bull call spread and the bull put spread. An investor should be vast in this two before making a choice.

a) Bull Call Spread Strategy

A bull call spread allows an investor to sell 1 Out of The Money call options and buy another In The Money call option. The call option that has a low strike price will be ITM while the call option with a higher strike price is OTM. The underlying security and expiry date should always be same for both calls. The overall effect of this strategy is to breakeven on a buy call strategy and bring down the cost. An investor utilizing this strategy can make profit only when the stock market prices go up. However, he makes a loss when the stock price falls below the lower strike.

For a moderately bullish investor, the risk is limited to the premium paid to obtain the position. Maximum loss occurs where the underlying stock falls remains at the low strike level. This investor receives rewards that are limited to the difference between the high strike and the low strike price less the net premium cost. Maximum profit occurs where the underlying stock rises to the level of the higher strike or above it. When the strike price of purchased call is added to Net debit paid, an investor gets the Break Even Point.

Example

An investor x buys a call with a strike price $ 4100 at a premium of 170.45, and sells the call option with a strike price $ 4400 at a premium of $ 35.40. The net debit here is $ 135.05, which is also his maximum loss.

Payoff schedule:

Call cost on expiry	Net payoff from call bought($)	Net payoff from call sold($)	Net Payoff ($)
3500.00	-170.45	35.40	-135.05
3600.00	-170.45	35.40	-135.05
3700.00	-170.45	35.40	-135.05
3800.00	-170.45	35.40	-135.05
3900.00	-170.45	35.40	-135.05
4000.00	-170.45	35.40	-135.05
4100.00	-170.45	35.40	-135.05
4200.00	-70.45	35.40	-35.05
4235.05	-35.40	35.40	0
4300.00	29.55	35.40	64.95
4400.00	129.55	35.40	164.95
4500.00	229.55	-64.60	164.95
4600.00	329.55	-164.60	164.95
4700.00	429.55	-264.60	164.95
4800.00	529.55	-364.60	164.95
4900.00	629.55	-464.60	164.95
5000.00	729.55	-564.60	164.95
5100.00	829.55	-664.60	164.95
5200.00	929.55	-764.60	164.95

The bull Call spread strategy drags down the Break Even Point, if the 4100$ strike price call is purchased the Break Even Point would have been 4270.75 reducing the cost of trade. Purchasing the 4100$ strike price call makes the cost of the trade to be 75.45, reducing the loss of the trade. This strategy has minimum gains making them suitable to venture in when the stock option market is moderately bullish. The following charts demonstrate moderately bullish strategy.

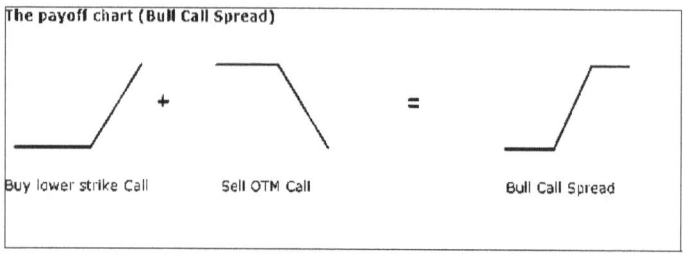

b) Bull Put Spread Strategies

This strategy generates profit when the stock option market is rising or at bound range. It aims to minimize the possible attainable losses that arise from a put sold by buying a lower strike put that is insurance for the put sold. The lower strike put purchased is more of an Out of The Money than the higher strike put option sold making it possible for the investor to receive a net credit from the purchased put. OTM is cheaper than the put option sold. This strategy is almost the same to the call spread but it does not generate the net premium and collect an income.

Both puts expire without any profit generation when the stock market rises and the investor can retain the premium. The investors breakeven point is the higher strike less the net credit received when the stock index falls. The investor will always make a profit if the underlying stock remains the same. If not, the investor makes a loss. We can get the maximum loss through getting the difference in the strikes and subtracting from the net credit received.

A moderately bullish investor risks a maximum loss when the underlying stock goes below the strike level or at its level. He profits when the net premium credit, Maximum profit occurs where underlying rises to the level of the higher strike or above.

Example

Mr. XYZ sells a Put option with a strike price of $ 4000 at a premium of $21.45 and buys a further OTM Put option with a strike price $ 3800 at a premium of $ 3.00 when the current is at 4191.10, with both options expiring on 31 July.

Buy puts and sell puts		
Put Index	Current value	4191.10
Sell put option	Strike Price	4000
Mr. XYZ Receives	Premium	21.45
Buy Put options	Strike Price	3800
He Pays	Premium	3.0
	Net premium Received	18.45
	Break Even Point	3981.55

Payoff schedule:

Call cost on expiry	Net payoff from call bought($)	Net payoff from call sold($)	Net Payoff ($)
3500.00	297.00	-478.55	-181.55
3600.00	197.00	-378.55	-181.55
3700.00	97.00	-278.55	-181.55
3800.00	-3.00	-178.55	-181.55
3900.00	-3.00	-78.55	-81.55
3981.55	-3.00	3.00	0.00
4000.00	-3.00	21.45	18.45
4100.00	-3.00	21.45	18.45
4200.00	-3.00	21.45	18.45
4300.00	-3.00	21.45	18.45
4400.00	-3.00	21.45	18.45
4500.00	-3.00	21.45	18.45
4600.00	-3.00	21.45	18.45
4700.00	-3.00	21.45	18.45
4800.00	-3.00	21.45	18.45

The strategy earns a net income for the investor as well as limits the downside risk of a Put sold. The chart below shows the payoff chart.

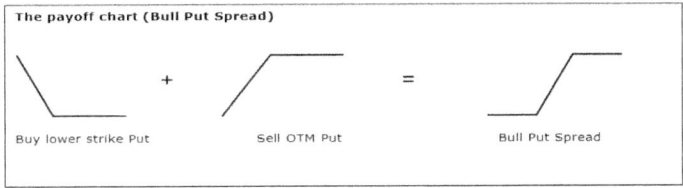

Long Combo: Sell A Put Buy A Call

A long combo entails, selling a lower risk put option and buying a higher strike call. It stimulates the act of buying a stock at a fraction of the stock price. The advantage of this strategy is that it is cheap. It pays off to a long stock; however, there are gaps between the strikes. As the stock price rises, the strategy generates profit. The risks and profits of a bullish investor on stock are unlimited and the Break Even Point is obtained when the high strike is added to the net debt.

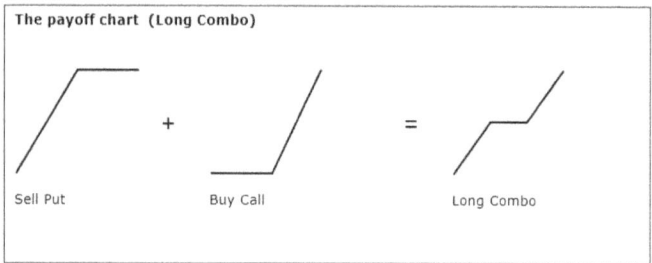

Synthetic Long Call

In this strategy, an investor acquires a stock because he feels bullish about it. If by chance the stock goes down, he wishes he had insurance against the fall price. He goes ahead to buy a Put on the stock to acquire the legality to sell the stock at the strike price. The strike price is the strike at which an investor acquired the stock or slightly below it, out of the money strike price. In case the price of the stock rises, he gets the full benefit of the price rise. If by chance the price of the underlying stock falls, the investor can trade the put option. This limits his loss as the Put option gives him an opportunity to freelance and stops further losses. It is a strategy with a limited loss and avails the opportunity for unlimited profit after subtracting the net put.

Note that the result of this strategy resembles a Call Option Buy but is different because an investor has taken an exposure to an underlying stock with the aim of holding it and exercising it with the benefits of price increase. At the same time, it is an insurance against very adverse price fluctuations.

An investor exercises the simple buying of a call option he wants to take advantage of price movement in the underlying stock but it lacks an underlying position in the stock. This strategy is used when ownership is desired of stock but the investor is concerned about downside risk in the recent future. He obtains risk by adding losses limited to Stock price to the Put Premium and subtracting the Put Strike price Break-even Point is equal to adding the Put Strike Price, Put Premium and Stock Price then subtracting the Put Strike Price.

Pay Off Chart For A Synthetic Long Call

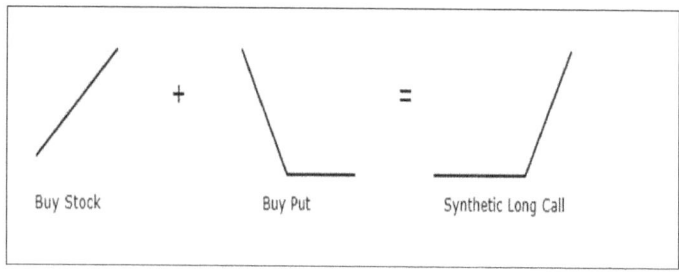

Conclusively, this is a low risk strategy that limits the loss if the market price falls and provides unlimited avenues of profit generation if the stock market rises. It is a good strategy when you buy a stock for medium or long-term purposes with the aim of protection against risk. The pay-off is similar to the call option bought.

2) Bearish Strategies

A trader is bearish when he expects the underlying stock to decrease thus, utilizes bearish strategies. The seller of a call has an obligation to sell the stock to the customer at a set hoping that the underlying stock price will fall. The put option buyer anticipates the price to drop so that he sells the stock at a higher price to the put option seller. A call option gives the proprietor the right to buy an asset at a set price before expiration but not the obligation to do the same. A put option gives the proprietor the right to sell the option before the expiration date. Moderate bearish traders choose prices for the expected deadline and utilize bear spread strategies to reduce risk. They usually cost less to employ. Mildly bearish trading strategies are options strategies that have the money making potential as long as the underlying stock price does not go up by the options expiration date. The most common Bearish strategies that yield profit with less risk are the Bear but spread and the bear call spread.

- **Bear Call Spread Strategy**

This strategy protects the downside of a call sold. The trader buys a call at a high strike price and sees to it that the call sells. He gets a net credit because the call he buys is of a higher strike price. He has to buy OTM call option and sell ITM call options on the underlying stock at the same time. This strategy is done with both Out of The Money calls with the call purchases being higher Out of The Money strikes than the sold call. If the stock index rises, the investor makes a profit otherwise, he makes a loss. These investors' risks are limited to the difference between the two strikes less the net premium. Their rewards are premiums received for the short call less the premium paid for the long call. He gets the Break Even Point is when by adding the Lower Strike to the net credit. Check the following example for a mild bearish investor.

A bearish trader sells an ITM call option with strike price of $ 2600 at a premium of $154 and buys an OTM call option with strike price $ 26800 as a premium of $49

When a trader Sells a call with a lower strike and buys with a higher strike		
call index	Current price	2694
Sell ITM call option	Strike Price($)	2600
He receives	Premium ($)	154
Buy OTM call option	Strike Price ($)	2800
He pays	Premium ($)	49
	Net premium received ($)	105
	Break Even Point($)	2705

Payoff schedule:

Call cost on expiry	Net payoff from call bought($)	Net payoff from call sold($)	Net Payoff ($)
2100	154	-49	105
2200	154	-49	105
2300	154	-49	105
2400	154	-49	105
2500	154	-49	105
2600	154	-49	105
2700	54	-49	5
2705	49	-49	0
2800	-46	-49	-95
2900	-146	51	-95
3000	-246	151	-95
3100	-346	251	-95
3200	-446	351	-95
3300	-546	451	-95

The payoff chart for a bear call spread

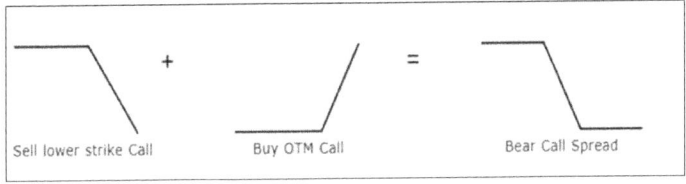

- **Bear Put Spread Strategy**

This strategy requires the investor to buy high put option and sell lower put option on the stock market before the expiratory date creating a net debit for the investor. The aim of the bear put spread strategy is to cut down on costs and increase the value of acquiring a put option. An investor gains rewards when the stock prices fall. The puts will have the effect of limiting the side down and the puts sold will reduce the expenses of a trader. If the stock price closes below the lower put Option, strike price increases above the higher put strike price at the expiration date, and then the investor Maximizes his loss.

When an investor is moderately bearish, his risk is limited to the net amount paid for the spread while his chances of winning are limited to the difference between the high and low strike prices less the premium paid. Subtracting the long put strike price from the premium paid gives the Break Even Point (BEP).

Example

A put index current price is at 2694, a trader expects the price to fall. He buys one ITM put with a strike price $ 2800 at a premium of $ 132 and sells another OTM put with strike price $ 2600 at a Premium $ 52 as summarized in the table below

Buy a single put with high strike and sell another with a lower strike.		
index	Current price	2694
Buy ITM put option	Strike Price($)	2800
Mr. xyz Receives	Premium ($)	132
sell OTM put option	Strike Price ($)	2600
Mr. xyz Receives.	Premium ($)	52
	Net premium received ($)	80
	Break Even Point($)	2720

The chart below shows a bear put spread.

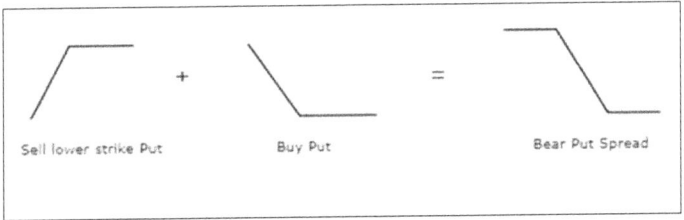

- **Short Call Strategy**

When an investor buys a call option hoping that the underlying stoke would rise and sells them when he expects the underlying stock to fall he is utilizing the short call strategy. A very bearish investor expects the market to fall to sell call options. He has limited potential of making profit and risks large lose on the underlying stock. Even though this strategy is not had to execute, the call seller has unlimited risks. When an investor is very aggressive and very bearish about the stock, he employs this strategy. He has unlimited risks and his rewards are limited to the amount of premium. By adding the strike price to the premium, we get The Break Even Point.

Example

A trader is bearish about the stock option market and expects it to fall. He sells a Call option with a strike price of $ 2600 and at a premium of $ 154, when the current call option is at 2694. If the call price stays at 2600 or below, the buyer will not exercise the Call option and the trader can retain the entire premium of $ 154.

The Pay Off Schedule And Chart For A Short Call

On expiry closes at	Net Payoff from the Call Options
2400	154
2500	154
2600	154
2700	54
2754	0
2800	-46
2900	-146
3000	-246

When trader uses this strategy when he is a go-getter who expects the expects the stock price to fall. It is a risky strategy since as the stock price rises, the short call loses money rapidly. If there is a fall in the stock market below, the strike price the loss is more significant. This strategy is also called Short Naked Call Since the investor does not own the underlying stock that he is shorting.

The Difference Between Bullish And Bearish Strategies

	Calls : Bullish strategies	Puts: Bearish strategies
Buyers	Hold the right to buy stock, anticipate a rise in the stock price.	They have the right to sell stock; they anticipate a decline in the stock option price.
Sellers	Have obligation to buy stoke they want stock price to rise	They have obligation to buy stoke, they want the stock price to fall.

3) Neutral Strategies

When an investor is not certain whether the underlying stock will rise or fall, he employs the Neutral strategies to trade options. Neutral strategies are indirect strategies because the probability of gaining profit does not depend on the underlying stock price fluctuation. The best neutral strategy to use on stoke option trade is dependent on the expected fluctuations of the underlying stock prices. Neutral trading strategies that are bullish on volatility yield reward when the underlying stock price either increases or decrease. They include the short butterfly and the short condor, the long straddle, long strangle, and long Calendar.

Neutral trading strategies that are bearish on volatility yield reward when the underlying stock price shows a little or no variation in prices. Such strategies include the long butterfly, short straddle, short strangle, the long calendar and long butterfly.

a) Butterfly Strategies

Butterfly strategies possess less risk, it is an option strategy without direction and is designed to elicit a higher probability of earning a limited profit when the future unpredictability of an underlying stock is expected to increase or decrease than the awaited fluctuation on the long term or short term respectively. The most common types in this strategy are the long and short butterfly.

Long Call Butterfly

An investor who expects very little movement in stock price applies this strategy. In this case, the investor is looking forward to profit from low volatility and at a reduced price. This strategy diversifies the risk reward ratio for the trader. A long butterfly resembles the short straddle except that loses are limited. This strategy is expected to make profit if the long-term volatility is lower than the awaited volatility. The option strategies can either be long call with a strike price, short call with a strike. This strategy is done by the buying strategy can be done by selling 2 ATM Calls, buying an ITM Call, and buying an OTM Call options. Equilibrium should exist between the three strike prices. If the stock remains range bound, the results are positive. The maximum reward in this strategy is restricted and takes place in the middle strike of expiry date in this strategy.

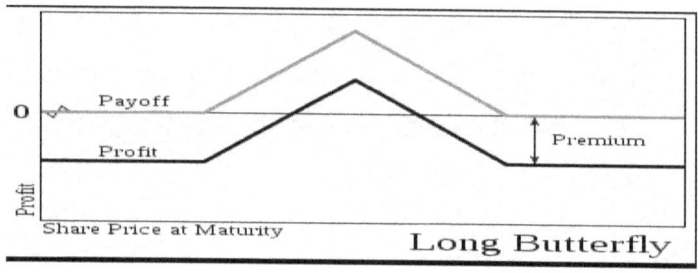

Long Butterfly

Short Butterfly Strategy

A short call butterfly is a strategy for volatile markets. It gives an investor a net credit by selling one low striking In The Money call, buying 2 In The Money calls and selling another high strike Out of The Money. An investor should try this income generation strategy; there should be equal distance between each strike. The resulting position will yield profit if there are big fluctuations on the market. The maximum risk occurs if the stock finishes on either side of the upper and lower strikes at the expiry date. However, this strategy offers small returns when compared to straddles. When an investor is neutral on the market and bullish on volatility, the risk is limited to the net difference between strike less the premium position. After receiving net Premiums from the option, spread the investor gets the reward. He has two breakeven points.

The Upper BEP is obtained when net premium received is subtracted from the high strike short call and gets the lower BEP when the Net premium received is subtracted from the lower strike short call. the chart below shows the result of a short call butterfly strategy.

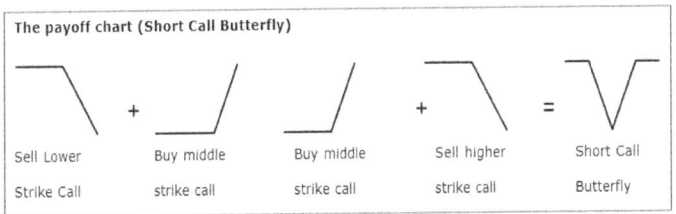

The payoff chart (Short Call Butterfly)

Sell Lower Strike Call + Buy middle strike call / Buy middle strike call + Sell higher strike call = Short Call Butterfly

b) Short Put Strategy

Bearish investors buy puts on the stock option market while bullish investors sell puts in the stock option market. Bullish investors expect the stock price to rise or remain constant at the minimum. When an investor sells a put option, he earns a premium. If the stock price goes above the strike price, the short put generates a profit for the seller by the amount of premium, since the buyer will not exercise the put option and the put seller can hold on to the premium of the stock price decreases below the strike price the put seller will lose the money. This investor calculates his risk by subtracting the put premium from the put strike price. The rewards are limited to the amount of premium received. The Break Even Point is obtained through subtracting the premium from the put strike price. Check the example below.

A trader is bullish on put option when it is at 4191.10. He sells a put at a price of 4100 a premium of $ 170.50 if the stock market is above 4100, he will gain the amount premium as the put buyer wound exercise this option. In this case, the put option falls below 4100, put buyer will trade the option and will start losing money. If the put option falls below the break Even Point that is 3929.50 then the investor will lose premium or even more depending on the extremity of the put price fall.

The payoff schedule and chart for a short put:

On expiry Closes at	Net Payof from the Put Option
3400.00	-529.50
3500.00	-429.50
3700.00	-229.50
3900.00	-29.50
3929.50	0
4100.00	170.50
4300.00	170.50
4500.00	170.50

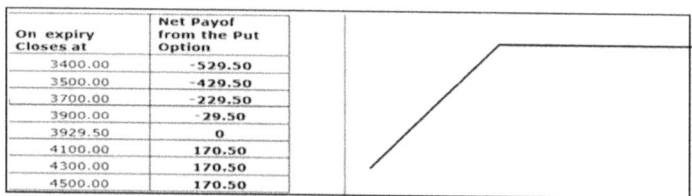

c) Long Put

Buying a put is the opposite of buying a call. Bullish investors invest their asset in buying calls, while bearish investors buy puts. A buyer gets the right to sell the underlying stock at a given time with minimum risks if he buys a put. A long put is a bearish strategy. The risk of this investor is limited to the amount of premium paid; the reward of this investor is unlimited. Subtracting stock point from the premium gives the investor his breakeven point.

An investor is bearish on a put option whose current price is 2694. On 24th June, he buys a Put option with a strike price $ 2600 and at a premium of $ 52 .it expiring on 31st July. If the put option goes below 2548, he will make a profit on exercising the option. In case option rises above 2600, he can forego the option meaning it expires worthless thus he incurs a maximum loss of the premium.

The payoff schedule and chart for a long put is illustrated below:

The payoff schedule		The payoff chart (Long Put)
On expiry closes at	Net Payoff from Put Option	
2300		
2400	148	
2500	48	
2548	0	
2600	-52	
2700	-52	
2800	-52	
2900	-52	

d) Covered Call Strategy

In this strategy, an investor owns stock options hoping it would rise largely in the long-term but not with a wide gap in the near future. The investor sells a call option on his underlying stock since he would like to earn some amount from the shares. The call option that earns him a premium is usually an OTM call. The investor resists exercising this option unless the stock price rises above the stock price. He remains the call seller and can hold on to the premium. A stock investor adopting this strategy is neutral and moderately bullish on the stock.

The investor buys a stock when he feels it is good for medium to long term but is neutral or bearish in the near future. At the same time, the investor confidently exits the stock market when he has hit his target. He can sell a call option at its strike price to earn a premium. His position is that of a call seller who owns underlying stock.

In case the stock price goes above the strike price, the call buyer who has the right to buy the stock at the strike price will exercise the call option. An investor who has to sell stock to a call buyer will sell the stock price at its stroke price and earns a premium on top of the strike price. In a call-covered strategy, every call option sold is replaced by a stock owned by the call seller. This strategy gives an increase in income as the stock price rises. See the covered call chart below.

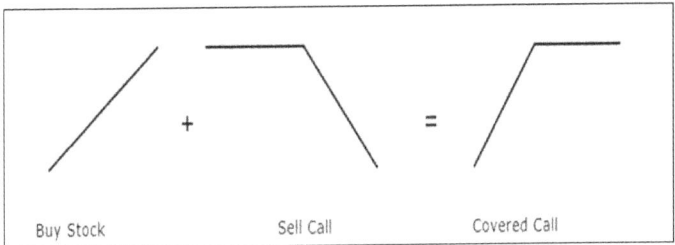

e) Protective Call Strategy

It is also known as synthetic long put. It is realized when an investor thinks they are out of stock, they buy more call options and store as the underlying stock to counter the sold call options. An Investor shorts a stock and buys an ATM or slightly OTM call. This investor creates a payoff as the net effect for utilizing this strategy just like in a long put but he has a net credit instead of having a net debt. If the stock price falls, the investor gains in the downward fall in price. When a sudden rise in the price of the stock comes about, the investor loses are limited. The payoff from the long call will increase countering the loss realized in value of the short stock position. This strategy retains downside profit potential and hedges the upside in the stock position.

It is used when the investor is bearish on the market but want insurance against unexpected rise in price of the stock. When you subtract the call strike price from the maximum call price and add premium, you will obtain the risk. You can get the reward through subtracting call premium from the maximum stock price. Stock price less call premium gives you the Break Even point

Synthetic long put payoff chart:

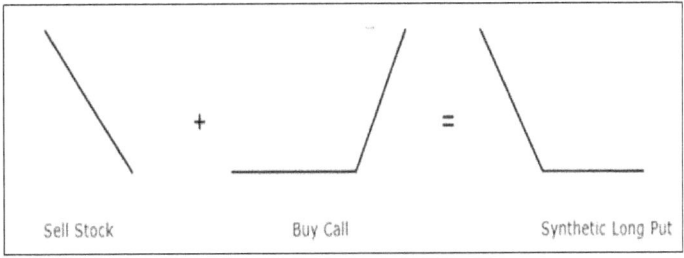

f) Long Straddle Strategy

An investor utilizes this strategy when he expects the stock market to move slowly. It includes the buying of puts with the same maturity period and strike price on the same stock market. An investor can take advantage on both upward and downward movement of the stock market. A call is exercised when the stock index rises and a decrease in price leads in the expiration of a put. Exercising the put leads to expiration of the call. Profit generation happens if the stock shows volatility to cover the cost of the trade. This trader is neutral in direction. The risk that he is likely to experience is limited to the premium that he pays. He has unlimited possibilities of rewards. We can get the Upper Break

Even Point by adding the Strike Price of Long Call to the Net Premium Paid and the Lower Break Even Point through subtracting the net premium from the Strike Price of Long Put.

Payoff chart for long straddle:

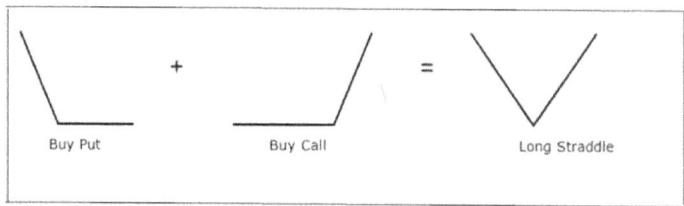

g) Short Straddle

When an investor feels the market will not show much movement. This is the opposite of a long straddle. He sells calls and puts on the same market from the same maturity and strike price. It results to a net income. If the stock does not move much in either direction, the investor retains the premium. This is because he exercises neither the put nor the call. If the stoke moves either up or down, the investor loses can be significant. A short Straddle is a risky strategy and an investor should be careful before making a choice. If the stock value stays close to the strike price on expire of the contracts, the investor receives premium (maximum gains). This investor has unlimited risks. He receives rewards limited to the premium he receives. We obtain the upper Break Even Point by adding the strike price of the short call to the net premium. The lower Break Even Point is the strike price of the short put less the net premium received.

Payoff chart for a short straddle:

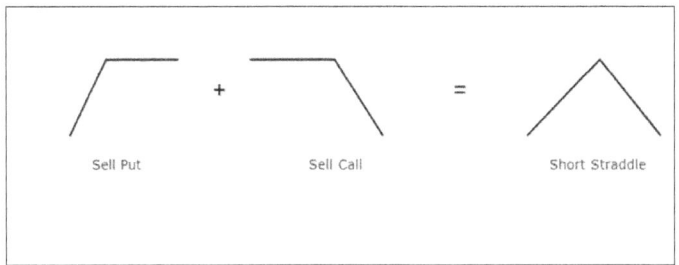

h) Long Call Condor Strategy

This strategy allows the investor to buy ITM call option in the lover strike, sell 1 ITM call option in the lower middle, Sell 1 OTM call Option In the higher Middle and buy IOTM call option in the High strike. The long options that are outside the strike ensure that the risk is limited on both sides. A long condor strategy can be likened to the long butterfly strategy but they differ in the strike prices between the two middle sold options. The pay off reward margin is wider in a long condor than in long butterfly. This strategy is applicable in a range bound market. When the stock market shows little volatility and the market remains range bound then the resulting position gives rewards. An investor maximizes his rewards if the stock breaks even between the middle strike prices at expiration.

This neutral strategy is applied when an investor believes that the underlying market will trade in a range with low volatility until the options expire. The investors' risks are limited to the minimum of the difference between the low strike call spread less the high call less the high call spread less the total premiums for the condor. He has limited rewards and may realize his maximum profit when he trades between the two striking prices. We calculate the upper Break Even Point by subtracting the net debit from the high strike. In addition, the low Break Even Point by Adding the lowest strike to the net debit.

Pay off chart for a long condor:

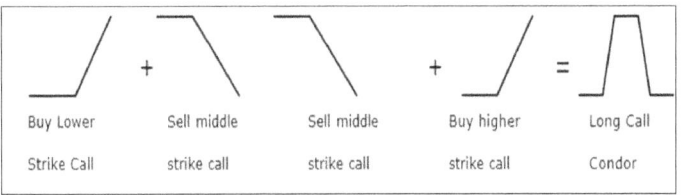

| Buy Lower Strike Call | Sell middle strike call | Sell middle strike call | Buy higher strike call | Long Call Condor |

i) Short Call Condor

This strategy allow an investor to sell a low strike-1IMT call, Buy 1 OTM call which is in the high middle, Buy 1 ITM call option lower middle and sell 1 OTM call option – high strike. Having the two middle bought options at different strike price is what makes the short condor different from the short butterfly strategy; when the stock market is very volatile and has big movements the investor can generates profit. The maximum Profit occurs if the stock finishes on either side of the upper or lower strike prices at expiration. This strategy is used when an investor believes that the market will break out of the trading range but not sure in which direction.

When an investor uses the short condor strategy, he has limited risks and benefits, The Maximum loss of a short condor occurs at the center of the option spread. When the underlying stock is trading past the upper or lower strike, an investor gets maximum profit.

An investor obtains the higher Break Even Point by subtracting the net credits from the high strike while the lower Break Even Point is obtained through adding the net credits to the lower strike price.

Payoff chart for a long condor strategy:

Sell Lower Strike Call	+	Buy middle strike call		Buy middle strike call	+	Sell higher strike call	=	Short Call Condor

j) Collar Strategy

This is the strategic buying of a Put to insure against the fall in the price of the stock market. This strategy is similar to the covered call strategy but presents with very limited risks. An investor of collar strategy buys the stock and insures against the downside- low strike price by acquiring a put and partially financing it by selling a call. The call sold is OTM while the put bought is ITM that has the same date of expiration. The put here counters the downside risk. On the other hand, this investor does not receive unlimited rewards because he has rights on the call.

Below is an illustration of a payoff chart:

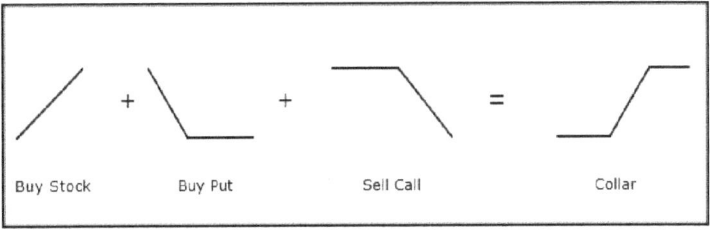

Chapter 4: Option Volume And Open Interest, Option Liquidity, And Option Time Value

Option Volume And Open Interest

The movement of price in option market is as a result of, decisions made by the millions of traders. Besides price movements there are statistics, which can inform you what the other market contributors are doing. We are going to look at two aspects that you need to consider while trading options. They are: option volume and open interest.

- **Option Volume**

This gives you important insight of the strength of the existing market, plus the direction of the option fundamental stock. The volume also known as market breadth is determined by shares. It informs you on how important price movement is in the market.

Bear in mind that trading volume is comparative; it needs to be contrasted with the average daily volume of stock that is in question. When we have a large percentage change of prices, followed by an even larger volume than normal, this is an indication of the strength of the market in relation to the direction of change. In cases where we have a large percentage increase of prices with small trading volumes. This tends not to show the direction of the market.

- **Open Interest**

As a trader you need to understand this concept. Although, it is not as important as option price, or the current volume, it provides very useful information that you need to consider in entering an option position. Most traders ignore open interest, yet it is always along, the ask price, bid price, implied volatility and volume.

Option trading creates a new option contract once a trade has been placed, while in stock trading there is a number of shares that ought to be traded. When it comes to open interest it tells you the total number of option contracts that are open. That is, there are contracts which have been traded and they are not liquidated either by an exercise or counteracting trade.

Importance Of Open Interest

- With open interest you are able to verify if there is a high or low volume of a particular option. This is possible by looking at the relative volume of traded contracts. For instance, if the volume exceeds an existing open interest for a particular day, this means that the trading of the option was very high on that day.

- It gives key information on the liquidity of an option. In instances where there is no open interest for an option, then there is also no secondary market for the option. If an option has a large open interest, it indicates that the option has generous number of sellers and buyers. Therefore, having a bigger option interest, the easier it is to trade the option in question at a reasonable spread.

The daily option volume and open interest can be utilized in order, to find trading ideas that could be overlooked. They are also important in making sure that the options you are trading are liquid. As a result, making it easy for you to enter and exit a trade and ensuring the best price possible for your options.

Relationship Between Open Interest And Volume In Line With Prices

1. A rise in the volume leads to a rise in the open interest, if the prices are rising which means that the market is strong.

2. A fall in the volume of an options results into a fall in the open interest, if the prices are rising. This indicates that the market is weakening.

3. In cases where the prices are falling. The volume and the open interest are rising indicates that the market is weak.

4. The falling in prices, volume and open interest shows that the market is strengthening.

How To Determine Option Liquidity

Liquidity is the ability to be able to enter or exit a trade with ease, if you are dealing with trading options and stock. You have a liquid instrument, when you have a lot of investors who are actively trading on a particular option or stock. On the other hand, we have illiquid, which is when there is limited number of people who are actively selling or buying stock or options.

You can take liquidity as a revolving door, that turns quickly thus allowing many opportunities to enter or exit a market. An illiquid market is a slow and unreliable revolving door, as it takes a lot of time to get through or it may even get stuck.

Aspects Of Liquidity To Consider When Placing A Trade

1. **Stock volume**

This is the amount of shares that is traded in a given day. While trading stocks, stocks that have a volume of more than 1,000,000 shares are traded. This shows that the bid/ask spread will be tight, thus enabling you to be able to enter and exit a trade at a fair price of the market.

A stock volume is not always the same with option volume. This is because you can trade stocks heavily but still have a barren market. This is important to keep in mind while trading.

2. Strike Price

In the case where options strike has a bigger amount of open interest, with a low volume. This could end up being a slow day for trading the precise strike price. This means you could have a considerate chance of either getting in or out of the trade.

However, if a strike has a low open market and a high volume, this means that the market participants are closing the options on the strike. Therefore, making it very difficult to be satisfied at a fair price of the market

3. Bid/ask Spread

Check the bid/ask spread to see if the fundamental stock is liquid. A bid/ask spread is the width of the sold stock or option and ask which is the bought option or stock. Having a tight bid/ask spread indicates that the stock or option is frequently traded.

It also shows that there is a lot of supply and demand of the fundamentals. Hence, allows you to obtain a fair market, which is greater for retail traders. A wide bid/ask spreads can at times indicate that the specific strike price of the fundamentals is illiquid.

To check if the underlying is liquid or if it's not, the underlying stock price is multiplied by (1/10) of 1%. Dough does this calculation for you. When you see a small orange teardrop, which is on the right of your leg trade. This indicates that the particular leg has a wider bid/ask spread of more than 1/10 of 1% of the stock price.

Getting a narrow bid/ask spread is important because it will affect the profitability of your stock. Also consider the amount of stock price which is expected to move against the bid/ask spread price options.

4. Open Interest

When it comes to option liquidity, you are able to see the open interest, also referred to as open option contract. Options have a predetermined expiration date. Therefore, they are not instantly traded as in the case of shares of stock. Open interest is larger than the option volume in numbers. It is able to indicate the amount of contracts that is open.

These aspects are put together to one term that is liquidity. This helps to determine if a particular fundamental is tradable.

Importance Of Liquidity

- You can get stuck in an unwanted position if your stock is illiquid.

- You can receive a partial amount for the trade if your stock is not liquid.

- Liquid options that are actively being traded have more expiration weeks and strikes plus months that you can choose from.

- Liquidity is very important for traders who are active in the fast market, for this is when the closing and opening of a position is a pressing issue.

More Understanding On Option Time Value

Time value is basically the price of risk paid so as to enable the option buyer the right to either sell or buy stock before the option expires. This can be considered as an insurance premium. The value of an option is determined by the total time value and the intrinsic value.

When there is a longer time to expiration, this means that the time value for an option is also more. At-The-Money options tend to have a high time value. This is because the high potential for intrinsic value increases a lot at this point. Here time value decreases considering movements of options to deeper ITM.

In case an option is a far Out-Of-The-Money, it will not command a high time value. This is because it has a lower chance of being In-The-Money. Options have a higher time value when the options are At-The-Money, for they have a higher chance of ending up to be In-The-Money.

In the event where the call strike price is below a current strike price, then the option is "deeply in the money". In the case where the strike price is above a current stock price, the option will be "far out of the money".

Moneyless is the association of the option's strike price to the current strike price of fundamental assets. You can obtain a cash flow by exercising an option. It will result to liquidating of the resulting stock position, then we can say that the option is "in the money"; if not it's "out of the money".

It is important to note that "moneyless" which can either be the property of being in the money or out of the money has absolutely nothing to do with an individual's loss or profit. Rather it is independent of the amount that is paid for an option. Therefore, it is useful as it describes the relationship there is between strike price and the stock price.

For put and call option, expiration is nearer when the time value decreases. They are the two variables that affect the time- value component of a given option. As the expiration gets closer, it increases the rate of decreasing time value. This usually happens in At-The-Money options. At these options, their time value decreases very fast especially in the last month before it expires.

We know that, the time value component of option's price decreases when the expiration date is drawing closer. The decreasing rate accelerates when the expiration date is at hand. This happens in both call and put options. This is also particular in At-The-Money options. This is an indication that the amount of time value for an option is disappearing from the option price in a day gets bigger as days pass by.

Why Intrinsic Value And Time Value Matters
- They help investors to be able to know what they are paying for in the event that they purchase an option. The intrinsic value represents the worth of an option in the event that the buyer exercises the option in the current time. Time value shows the possibility of an

option increasing in price before its expiration time. As a result, the mentioned factors help investors to be able to understand the rewards and risks of options.

- If an investor buys an ATM or an OTM option and the premium is equivalent to the time value; there is a higher risk of the option being worthless when its expiration date is reached at.

- When purchasing an ITM option, you are at a lower risk of the option becoming worthless at its expiration date, for it already has value. This is shown in the option's premium which has the time value and the intrinsic value. The option has a higher premium, because it has a lesser risk.

- A greater risk comes with greater rewards such as, OTM and ATM have greater risks but they also have a greater percent gains in profit compared to ITM options.

Note that for any particular expiration date given, the option which has the highest time value will be At-The-Money options. Also that the farthest an option's strike price is from the given current strike price, which can be from either direction the less time value it will have.

Chapter 5: Last Tips

Stock options can help you to gain big return in the stock market, or in some cases it can destroy your account completely. Hence trading them can be a great thing so long as you can comfortably handle your risk.

The 3 things that can help you increase your chances to be profitable are as followed.

i) Only Use A Small Percentage

You should only use a small percentage of your account on any option trade, this will help you reduce the total amount you can lose. This is a very effective strategy bearing in mind how fast option move. In case it happens that you end up on the wrong side of the trade, it's always good to lose as little as possible. When it comes to trading the most important thing is controlling your risk.

ii) Trade With The Trend

Always make sure that when you are trading you are trading with the existing trend. An object that is in motion will always stay in motion. There are high chances that when stocks are trending in a certain direction, it will continue trending in that direction at least for a while.

iii) Setting Targets

It is very important to have 2 targets, one target should tell you where/when to get out of option if you are right and the other one should be the one to tell you where to get out of an option when you are wrong. Thereby allowing you to reduce how much you can lose if the stock happens to turn against you, and in case you are right it allows you to get out if you think most of the moves have already been made.

An added side benefit to having targets is that it allows you to develop a risk to reward system and determine how much possible reward you want to take for every $1 you risk. Traders can gain profit through the volatility of the underlying stocks or securities over some period of time. Always invest wisely when it comes to option trading. Select the best strategy that fits you well. As an investor, invest in stock options that will allow you to make use of your capital in a better way.

www.ingramcontent.com/pod-product-compliance
Lightning Source LLC
Chambersburg PA
CBHW070346230526
45471CB00006B/2436